Henry M. Hervey

Pioneer Pamphlets

Henry M. Hervey

Pioneer Pamphlets

ISBN/EAN: 9783337149468

Printed in Europe, USA, Canada, Australia, Japan

Cover: Foto ©ninafisch / pixelio.de

More available books at **www.hansebooks.com**

OUR PIONEERS:

BEING BIOGRAPHICAL SKETCHES OF

CAPT. ELIAS HUGHES, JOHN RATLIFF,
BENJAMIN GREEN, RICHARD PITZER,
JOHN VAN BUSKIRK, ISAAC AND
JOHN STADDEN, AND CAPT.
SAMUEL ELLIOTT;

WITH BRIEF NOTICES OF THE

PIONEERS OF 1801 AND 1802:

BY ISAAC SMUCKER,

Sec'y of the Licking County Pioneer Society.

ALSO, A PAPER ON THE

PIONEER WOMEN OF THE WEST,

BY REV. MRS. C. STRINGER.

CONCLUDING WITH A POEM, ENTITLED

THE PIONEERS OF LICKING,

BY A. B. CLARK, Esq.,

Editor Newark American.

NEWARK, OHIO:
Clark & King, Printers. American Office.
1872.

Be it ours to gather from still living witnesses, and preserve for the future annalist, the important records of the teeming and romantic Past : to seize, while yet warm and glowing, and inscribe upon the page which shall be sought hereafter, the bright visions of song, and the fair images of Poetry, which gild the gloom and lighten the sorrows of the ever-fleeting Present : and thence draw lessons to fit us for and light to guide us through the shadowy but unknown Future!

CONTENTS.

Our Pioneers.

CAPT. ELIAS HUGHES and JOHN RATLIFF.
1798.

BIOGRAPHY, or the history of the life and character of an individual, is history, substantially. The acts, achievements, exploits and adventures of individual characters make the chief items of our history. This is pre eminently true of a newly settled country like ours, and of the first settlers—the pioneers of it. And most especially is this the fact of such a country as the territory northwest of the Ohio was, where the subjugation of the hostile savage tribes was the condition precedent to its permanent settlement. *Most emphatically our pioneers made our early history.* The delineation of characteristics and peculiarities; the narrations of actions, experiences, achievements, adventures; the bringing to public view the personal significance of those who played a distinguished part in "Life's drama," or were instrumental in the development of principles, is biography—and history, too. To trace a human life, (says a late writer,) to remark the manifold efforts, defeats, triumphs, perplexities, attainments, joys and sorrows which fill the space between the cradle and the grave, is the province of biography. Its importance and interest will, therefore, I trust, be apparent to all, and that these personal sketches will meet with kind appreciation.

Elias Hughes and John Ratliff were our first settlers, and closed their lives here, hence their names are as much interwoven with the history of Licking county as is the name of General Washington with the history of the United States, or as are the names of President Lincoln and General Grant with the history of the late rebellion. And to attempt the production of a history of our county without making Hughes and Ratliff prominent actors therein, would manifestly issue in failure.

Elias Hughes was born near the South Branch of the Potomac, a section of country which furnished Licking county many of its early settlers and most useful citizens. His birth occurred sometime before Braddock's defeat in 1755. Of his early life little is known, until in 1774 we find him a soldier in the army of General Lewis, engaged in the battle of Point Pleasant. General Lewis, you are aware, commanded the left wing of the army of Lord Dunmore, who was then Governor of the colony of Virginia, and successfully fought the distin-

guished Shawanese Chief, Cornstalk, who had a large force of Indians under his command. One-fifth of Lewis' command was killed or wounded, but Elias Hughes escaped unhurt in this hard-fought battle, which lasted an entire day. At the time of his death, which occurred more than seventy years after the battle, he was, and had been for years, the last survivor of that sanguinary conflict.

We next find Hughes a resident of Harrison county, in Western Virginia, where his chief employment, during the twenty-one years that intervened between the battle of Point Pleasant and the treaty of Greenville in 1795, was that of a scout or spy, on the frontier settlements near to or bordering on the Ohio river. This service, which was a labor of love with him, be rendered at the instance of his State and of the border settlers that had been for a long time greatly harassed by the Indians, who had murdered many of the whites on the frontiers, their women and children included, under circumstances of atrocity but seldom paralleled. Hughes' father, and others of his kindred, and also a young woman to whom he was betrothed, had been massacred by them. These acts of atrocious barbarity made him ever after an unrelenting and merciless enemy of the whole race of Red Skins; and in retaliation for their numerous butcheries, his deadly rifle was brought to bear fatally upon many of their number in after years. It is but an act of simple justice to the memory of this veteran pioneer, who was well known as an Indian-hater, and an Indian-killer, that the provocations he had, be fully presented, and properly understood. Born and raised on the frontiers, among a rude and unlettered people, and untaught and wholly uncultivated and unenlightened as he was, it is not surprising that, under all these circumstances, considering, too, the horrid aggravation he had, he should have given rather full play to strong and

malignant passions, and that he should have cherished, even to old age, the harsher and more revengeful feelings of his nature. His vindictiveness or sense of justice led him to keep accounts about balanced between the whole race of red men and himself. This he did, fully, so long as the Indians maintained a hostile attitude towards the whites—perhaps a little longer. He owed them nothing at the final settlement.

The treaty of Greenville, commonly called "Wayne's Treaty," made and ratified in 1795, terminated Indian hostilities, or rather the defeat of the Indians the previous year, by General Wayne, in the battle of the "Fallen Timbers," near the Rapids of the Maumee, brought about that result, and hence scouts were no longer required. Elias Hughes, like the Moor in Shakspeare when he reached the conviction that "Othello's occupation's gone," now finding his services as a scout no longer in demand, surrendered his commission of Captain of scouts, and directed his attention to more pacific and less hazardous pursuits. And here it may be stated that he had been commissioned by that distinguished frontiersman, Col. Ben. Wilson, the father of our fellow-citizen, Daniel Wilson, and of the late Mrs. Dr. John J. Brice, as a Captain of scouts.

In 1796 Hughes entered the service, as a hunter, of a surveying party who were about to engage in running the range lines of lands lying, in part, in what is now Licking county. The fine bottoms of the Licking were thus brought to his notice, and he resolved to leave his mountain home in the "Old Dominion," and locate himself and family on the uncultivated and more fertile lands of the Licking valley, beyond the white settlements. Accordingly, in the spring of 1797, he gathered together his limited effects, and with his wife and twelve children started for the mouth of the Licking, most of them going on foot, and the remainder on pack horses. This point

had been made accessible to footmen and horseback travelers by the location and opening in the year before, by Zane and others, the road from Wheeling to Maysville; and also of a road previously cut out from Marietta up the Muskingum river. John Ratliff, who was a nephew of Hughes, came with his wife and four children, with the latter, and in the same manner to the mouth of the Licking. Here they remained one year, and in the spring of 1798 both families, numbering twenty-one persons, moved in the same style to the "Bowling Green," twenty miles up the Licking from its mouth, and there made the first permanent white settlement in the territory now forming Licking county. They erected their cabins near the mouth of the Bowling Green Run, about four miles below Newark, on the banks of the Licking, and about half a mile, or less, apart. They found the "Bowling Green" a level, untimbered green lawn or prairie, and they at once proceeded to raise a crop of corn. Whether the "Bowling Green" was a natural prairie or had been cleared by the Indians or some white persons remains an unsettled question. The nearest neighbors of Hughes and Ratliff, for two years, lived about ten miles down the Licking, one of whom was Philip Barrick, who, in 1801, moved up the valley and located near the "Licking Narrows."

The Hughes and Ratliff colony subsisted mainly on the meat of wild animals of the forest, and on the fish caught and "*gigged*" in the Licking, although a considerable crop of vegetables and corn was raised the first and subsequent years. The elk and buffalo had disappeared, but bear, deer, wild turkies and a great variety of the smaller game, as well as fish, were in such abundance as to supply the full demands of these early settlers. Berries, wild fruits, nuts, and other spontaneous productions of the earth also contributed, for many years, in no inconsiderable degree to the subsistence of the pioneer settlers.

Ratliff, in some particulars, was a different style of man from Hughes. He was much more given to the peaceful avocations of life, and for one reared on the frontiers, had not been largely engaged in border warfare, though he, as well as Hughes, was considerably devoted to the chase, to fishing, trapping, bee hunting, as well as to the pursuit of the ferocious animals of the forest, and the birds of prey that tenanted this wilderness.

In 1799 a son was born to Elias Hughes, and he was the only accession to the Bowling Green colony in that year. In the year 1800, Benjamin Green, Richard Pitzer, Isaac Stadden, Samuel Elliott and John Stadden settled in the Licking valley, between Newark and the Bowling Green, and John Van Buskirk located in the South Fork valley, now Union township. John Larabee, James Maxwell and others came in the spring of 1801. Of these pioneers I will have more to say.

In the year 1801 an event of no inconsiderable importance transpired at the "Bowling Green." Two Indians came along one night and stole four horses. They belonged to Elias Hughes, John Ratliff, John Weedman, a recent emigrant, and a Mr. Bland who lived at the mouth of Licking, but who was at this time visiting Hughes. In the morning after their horses were stolen, their owners determined to pursue and kill the thieves, feeling assured that they were Indians. Weedman backed out, but Hughes, Ratliff and Bland, being well armed, started in pursuit. They were enabled to follow the trail, readily tracking them through the grass and weeds. Overtaking them on Owl creek they shot them. Bland's flint did not strike fire, but Hughes and Ratliff's did, and those Indians stole no more horses. When the Indians were overtaken and it was evident that the horses would be recovered, Bland

and Ratliff relented, and feeling less sanguinary than when they started on the pursuit, they suggested to Hughes to let the thieves escape, after the horses were obtained, but the latter was not that style of man. He negatived their proposition in such emphatic terms, and in the use of such forcible expletives of the profane order as were common among frontiersmen in those days, as to soon bring them to the determination with which they set out. When Hughes said a thing must be done, and he could do it, or cause it to be done, it was done. This was one of those cases—he had his way—they had agreed to kill the Indian horse thieves—*and they did!* Hughes knew them and believed them to have been engaged in stealing horses and then returning them to their owners for a compensation in skins and furs.

This sanguinary transaction necessitated the erection of a block-house on the "Bowling Green" as a means of protection against the infuriated friends of the defunct horse thieves, who were greatly incensed against those they suspected of killing them, but it never became necessary to defend it, the Indians finally deciding it inexpedient to assault it. One evening, however, after the excitement had nearly subsided, two well armed Indians entered Hughes' cabin and in a menacing manner introduced the subject of the killing of those Indians. Mrs. Hughes seeing that trouble might be had with their visitors, quietly sent for Ratliff who readily responded, rifle in hand. Hughes in those days always carried a butcher knife in his belt, and he also had a rifle at hand. Bloody work seemed imminent, but the Indians, after remaining face to face with those veteran back-woodsmen all night, sometimes in rather spirited discussion, deemed it wise, in the early morning, to retire without any hostile act.

John Weedman we naturally conclude lacked pluck. He was a Pennsylvanian, recently arrived. Before leaving his native State he had been hurried into an unwilling matrimonial arrangement on his part, and had abandoned his wife. The son that was soon born to him very narrowly escaped birth in wedlock. Weedman, some years later, purchased a farm near the southern borders of our county, and accumulated considerable property. He died in 1835 with the general belief of his neighbors that he was a bachelor. The aforesaid son, however, came on and obtained legal possession of the estate of his father, whom he never saw. For whatever else of romance there was in the life and adventures of John Weedman, who would not join in the agreed-upon enterprize of pursuing the thievish Indians, can be found in Pioneer Paper No. 17, by Dr. Wilson.

A word as to Bland. He removed from Pendleton county, Virginia, in 1798, with a wife and four children, coming some hundreds of miles over the Alleghany mountains on pack-horses to Marietta, following blind bridle paths and Indian trails a portion of the way. On reaching the mouth of Licking he took refuge with his family in a sugar camp. Before he had time to build a cabin he had born to him, in this sugar camp, a son whom they rocked in a sugar trough, which was then and there the best cradle that was accessible. Mr. Silas Bland, now in his seventy fifth year, who lives in Perry township, is this child of sugar-camp and of sugar-trough notoriety. A venerable and respectable pioneer, too, is this sugar camp and sugar trough baby of 1798. He is the oldest person now living in Licking county who was born in the valley of the Licking. His father, who pursued the horse thief Indians, possessed all the constituent elements of a first class pioneer, and after acting well his part he finally died in Muskingum county, where he had so long lived.

In 1802 Elias Hughes was elected

Captain of the first company of militia raised within the present limits of our county. This company he commanded a number of years. They had to go to Lancaster to attend battalion drills. Captain Hughes had four children born to him after he settled at the "Bowling Green," making the sum total of his children sixteen. Jonathan is the only one of the sixteen now living in Licking county. He was born in Harrison county, Virginia, in 1796, was brought to the mouth of Licking in 1797, and was two years old at the time of his father's removal in 1798 to the "Bowling Green." The older children had to walk, on their removal up the Licking, but Jonathan and his brother David, (who also was too young to walk) were brought up in a salt sack thrown across a horse. Jonathan was put in one end of the sack and David in the other, openings being first cut in the sack for their heads to go through. The sack was then slung across the pack saddled horse, and a rider or two, with other loading, put upon him and then started for the "Bowling Green," while the others walked or came up in a canoe. It would, indeed, be an interesting picture that gave us, on canvass, an accurate view of this original colony of emigrants while in motion. Jonathan, the salt sack boy of 1798, is now more than seventy-six years old, and is the oldest settler of our county—emphatically, our Pioneer.

Ratliff's wife died in 1802, and was, probably, the first white adult person that died within the present limits of our county. The only probable exception being that of a Mrs. Jones who died about the same time on the Munson farm, in Granville township, four miles west of Newark, where her husband, John Jones, had erected the first cabin in the township, being the one in which she died. Ratliff married again, his second wife being the daughter of a pioneer by the name of Stateler, who lived near the mouth of the Rocky Fork. He also raised a considerable family but none of them now live, if living at all, in our county. He had a son in the army during the war of 1812, who, after his return from the army, removed to Louisiana. He also had a daughter, Mary, who intermarried with a Mr. Evans. Some of the issue of this marriage, being grand-children of John Ratliff, are still living in our county, principally, I learn, in Perry township.

Ratliff finally removed to the south side of the Licking, near the mouth of the Brushy Fork, where he died about the year 1811. He, no more than Hughes, seems to have had much success in the acquisition of property. Indeed, it is not probable that either of them ever had much ambition in that direction.

Captain Elias Hughes, on all other subjects except Indian warfare, was generally of a taciturn disposition; but he was fond of relating his exploits and successes as a scout, sitting up whole nights, sometimes, to relate to willing, interested listeners his hair-breadth escapes and adventures, and the thrilling stories, heroic acts and deeds of renown in which he had borne a part. He was unassuming, temperate, honest, mild-mannered, unpretending, unambitious, but firm, determined, unyielding, and some thought him vindictive. When he resolved on a certain line of conduct he commonly pursued it to success, or failed only after a vigorous effort. Fond of adventure, he displayed in border warfare, in battle, in pursuit of Indians, and in explorations of new countries, and in the pioneer settlement of them, the energy, bravery, self-sacrificing virtues that so conspicuously distinguished the early pioneers of the Great West.

In the war of 1812 Capt. Hughes, notwithstanding his age, volunteered for the defense of Fort Meigs. On the formation of a company for that service, he was elected to conduct the men to headquarters at Worthington, for organization. At the election of company officers he was

made a Lieutenant, the late General John Spencer being elected Captain. He was patriotic to the core and so were his sons, not less than three of them being engaged in the same war. One of them contracted disease while in the service of his country, of which he died.

Elias Hughes lived many years on the North Fork, a few miles above Newark, and also for several years at Clinton, in Knox county, from whence he removed to Monroe township, near Johnstown. Here, in 1827, Mrs. Hughes died. She had the qualities which admirably adapted her to discharge the duties of a pioneer wife and mother. Her training had been in the Presbyterian faith, and the instruction to her children was in accord with it. Upon her death, most of his children having married and removed from the county, Captain Hughes became a welcome inmate of the house of his son, Jonathan, who lived in Utica. He, you remember, was introduced to you as the salt sack emigrant of 1798.

For many years Captain Hughes was a pensioner, regularly receiving from his beneficent government the means to enable him to spend his declining years in the full enjoyment of all the blessings of life, kindly ministered unto him by Jonathan and his family, with whom he spent the last seventeen years of his life.

Captain Hughes was the subject of more varied vicissitudes, adverse fortunes, and experiences more diversified than usually fall to the lot of man, but he met them in the heroic spirit of those who are determined to encounter them successfully, and meet the stern realities of life like men. Enduring as he did, for the last sixteen years of his life, the terrible affliction of total blindness, he was, of course, deprived of the enjoyments afforded by views of the glory and grandeur of the Creator's works; but he was resigned to this afflictive dispensation of Providence, feeling disposed to endure all meekly, calmly, patiently, and to trustingly, hopefully "bide his time."

In his declining years his attention was directed to religious subjects to which he gave much thoughtful and serious consideration, and for many years he cherished the cheering hopes of a happy future, inspired alone by the Christian's faith. He died in December, 1844, and was buried with military honors and other demonstrations of respect. His age is not certainly known, but the best information attainable makes him at the time of his death about ninety years old.

Such was the life and career, thus imperfectly sketched, of one of the most remarkable men that ever lived in our county. His was a life full of privations, adventures, hardships, toils, exposures, excitements, anxieties—a life Providentially preserved through so many years of constant peril, and of exposures to unusual hazards and dangers. It is one of our chief duties, as a Pioneer Society, to preserve from oblivion the recollection of the heroic deeds and achievements of our pioneer settlers; and to keep fresh and green in our memories, and in the memories of those who are to come after us, the sufferings and noble deeds of the self-sacrificing men and women who first settled in these forests, erected cabins, cleared the land, and converted the wilderness into fruitful fields, and made comfortable and pleasant homes for their descendants, the men and women of the present generation. And none of all the meritorious pioneers of our county are better entitled to this service at our hands than Captain Elias Hughes and John Ratliff, and their wives and children, who composed the colony of twenty one, that made the first settlement in the territory that now forms Licking county.

BENJAMIN GREEN and RICHARD PITZER.

1800.

The two families of Hughes and Ratliff were the sole occupants of the territory which now constitutes the county of Licking, at the close of the last century. Early in the spring of the opening year (1800) of the present century, however, three more (Green's, Pitzer's and Van Buskirk's) were added to their number, and so remained until August, when Isaac Stadden came with his family, making the sixth; and in September, Captain Samuel Elliott arrived, which made our seventh family. The marriage of Colonel John Stadden and Betsey, daughter of the aforesaid Green, which took place on Christmas day, 1800, made the eighth family, which was our whole number when the year closed.

In the spring of 1799, Benjamin Green, a revolutionary soldier, and his son-in-law, Richard Pitzer, left Allegheny county, Maryland, to settle in the Northwest Territory. On reaching the neighborhood of Marietta they decided to remain there a year and raise a crop, thus postponing, for a brief period, their removal farther westward.

Early in the spring of 1800 they removed their families to Shawnee Run, locating about two miles east of the junction of the North and South Forks of the Licking river, on the farm now owned by Rev. P. N. O'Bannon. They moved their families with some of their personal property on seven pack horses from Marietta to the mouth of Licking; while the flour of fifteen bushels of wheat, the "running gears" of a large wagon, and other bulky articles of household property were brought up the Muskingum, to the same point, in a large canoe, which made two voyages. Mr. Pitzer had charge of the pack-horse train, while Mr. Green, aided by a Mr. John Kelly and his son, Richard, then a boy of fifteen, run the canoe. The women and smaller children were mounted on the pack-horses, while all the boys that were large enough (except Richard) assisted Mr. Pitzer in the management of his train and in driving some domestic animals. At the mouth of the Licking they put their wagon together, and with it and the pack-horses came up the Licking to Shawnee Run. As their's was the first wagon to enter the territory which forms the county of Licking, they were compelled to cut out the road for it most of the way. This canoe-boy, Richard, who navigated the Muskingum river in the year 1800, and came up the Licking with the first wagon that entered our county, has been too feeble to unite in active co-operation with his fellow-pioneers in their public exercises, but has rendered essential service in furnishing facts connected with the early settlement of our county, especially of the Hog Run and Licking Valleys, which came under his own observation.

Messrs. Green and Pitzer remained two years at Shawnee Run, and then purchased land on Hog Run, and moved upon it. Mr. Pitzer died there in 1819, and his children removed to Illinois afterwards. Mr. Green remained on, or in the vicinity of the farm that he purchased in 1802, until his death, which occurred in 1835, when he was seventy-six

years of age. Mrs. Green died in 1822. They ha I fourteen children, eleven of whom were born before their arrival at Shawnee Run, and three afterwards. John Green, one of the sons, was an extensive contractor on the Ohio Canal, and is still living near Ottawa, in Illinois, at the advanced age of more than four score years. He led a very active, industrious life, and acquired a large fortune. Isaac, another son, was a man of intelligence and worth who represented Licking county several sessions in the State Legislature, being elected in 1841 and 1842. Richard, one of those fourteen children, has just deceased, at the advanced age of eighty-seven years, after a residence of seventy-two years in Licking county. Daniel, another son, lives near Hebron. The first sermon preached within the present limits of this county was preached at the Shawnee Run cabin of Mr. Green, probably a short time before his removal to Hog Run in the spring of 1802. Rev. Mr McDonald, a Presbyterian, was the preacher. And Mr. Green's cabin was found in 1803 by that distinguished itinerant pioneer Methodist, Rev. Asa Shinn, who made it a preaching place throughout the year that he had charge of Hock-Locking circuit. He organized a society at Mr. Green's in 1804, which was the first religious society or church organized in the territory which now constitutes Licking county. Mrs. Green and her daughter Sarah, Richard Pitzer and his wife, and John Stadden and Jacob Swisher, both sons-in law, with their wives, composed about all the members of this family-church when first organized. Mr. Benjamin Green was, or sometime after became a Baptist, and during a number of the closing years of his life he frequently exercised his gifts as a minister of that denomination. He never took charge of a church, I believe, but responded to occasional calls for his services as requisitions were made upon him for his ministerial labors.

Rev. Benjamin Green, in 1823, contracted a second marriage with Martha, widow of David Lewis, who was the daughter of that veteran pioneer of the 'Welsh Hills, Mr. Theophilus Rees. She survived him, and died at an advanced age.

Rev. Benjamin Green, though unlettered, is said to have been a man of some force in the pulpit, who presented his theological views to the public with considerable volubility and animation. He was an energetic, enterprising, useful pioneer, and in all the varied relations of life he met and discharged the duties devolved upon him with fidelity and honor. I regret that I am without information as to the career of this veteran pioneer before he left his mountain home amidst the Alleghenies in western Maryland, in 1799, with his wife and eleven children, to seek a home in the wilderness of the Northwest Territory. But it may be assumed that he practiced the virtues, and led the life of activity and usefulness that characterized him later in life. He acted well the pioneer's part and is entitled to the pioneer's honor.

Richard Green, of whom mention has been made as the canoe-boy of the Muskingum of the year 1800, lived here seventy two years, died in Licking township, April 16th, 1872, at the advanced age of eighty-seven years. He had lived here a longer time than any other person, except Colonel Jonathan Hughes, the salt-sack boy of 1798.

Richard Green was an observing, intelligent man, and a member, during many of the years of his long life, of that little Methodist Church on Hog Run, whose organization, the first in our county, he witnessed in the year 1804, by Rev. Asa Shinn, as before stated. Long let us cherish the memory of the useful and respected pioneers of those early years.

What great events transpired during the life-time of this veteran pioneer! He was born soon after the close of the revolution and

before the commencement of the constitutional history of our country—before General Washington was elected President. His father's family was the third that settled within the present limits of Licking county, when it was part of Ross county, Northwest Territory, Chillicothe being the county seat, and General St. Clair the Governor. Richard Green, our veteran pioneer, therefore, passed through all the phases of frontier life during the seventy-two intervening years between his boyhood and his old age. He led an industrious, useful, virtuous life, practicing the manly virtues and cultivating the Christian graces,

his end, therefore, was peace. In hope and resignation his earthly career of so many eventful years closed at the residence of his son, Rev. Benjamin Green, with whom his latter days were passed contentedly, happily. Living in harmony with the laws of his physical nature he naturally reached a good old age. Very unobtrusively, quietly, he ran off his more than eight decades of "mortal coil," and passed on into the sleep of death with calm lines of peacefulness upon his countenance, while his spirit doubtless floated happily on to a bright, a joyous awakening.

JOHN VAN BUSKIRK.

1800.

In the spring of the year 1800, and probably not a week after the advent of Green and Pitzer at Shawnee Run, John Van Buskirk arrived and entered upon a tract of land of thirty-one hundred acres on the South Fork, in what is now Union township. He had previously purchased it, and at once commenced erecting his buildings, clearing land and raising crops. Mr. Van Buskirk was born in the State of New Jersey, and came with his father's family in 1780 to Brooke county, Virginia, where he grew to manhood, and where, also, he married and lived until his removal to the South Fork, as above stated. He was a man of liberal means, being pecuniarily in more independent circumstances than any of our early-time settlers. He came to his new home in the wilderness (by way, principally, of the "Zane trail," as far as Brush Creek in Fairfield county,) with a full supply of wagons and domestic animals, and made the fifth settler within the present limits of Licking county.

Mr. Van Buskirk was a stout, active, resolute man and a woodsman and rifleman of the first order, frequently accompanying such frontier chieftains as Captain Samuel Brady and John McCulloch in their expeditions against the Indians. He acted well his part as a faithful, ever-ready, efficient pioneer on the frontiers of Virginia in giving protection to the settlers that were endeavoring to establish themselves in permanent homes on both sides of the Ohio river, and in the settlements bordering thereon, during the twenty years of Indian warfare that he spent at or near the mouth of Buffalo Creek, in Brooke county, Virginia. And most of those years in that region were years of fierce conflicts, of murderous warfare, of barbarity, blood and carnage.

John Van Buskirk remained on his farm, on the South Fork, until 1804, when he removed to Newark and rebuilt the Petticord & Belt mills, which he run, persistently, much more to the benefit of the public than himself, until near his

death. He died on the last day of December, 1840, at the age of almost eighty-five years. He was in the earlier part of his eventful, adventurous life, a man of great enterprise and force of character, and while living on the frontiers on the borders of the Ohio river, in common with his fellow-frontiersmen, he endured many hardships and privations, and had many hair-breadth escapes in the pursuit of marauding parties of Indians, and in his conflicts with them. As a spy he was invaluable to the frontier settlers. He scouted extensively between the Ohio and Tuscarawas rivers. Courage and patriotism were his distinguishing characteristics.

John Van Buskirk had a numerous family, but only one of his children (Rachel) is still living. His son John, who was an infant at the time of his removal to the South Fork valley in 1800, died last year, at his residence in Newark.

Mr. Van Buskirk was the first family to enter the territory which now forms Licking county, from the southeast, with a wagon. He left the "Zane trail" east of Lancaster, and cut a road from there to his land on the South Fork, in the spring of 1800, and was preceded by Green and Pitzer only a few days, who came up the Licking valley from the mouth of the Licking with a wagon, cutting out the road for that purpose most of the way up the valley to Shawnee Run, below Newark. Van Buskirk was then here, as stated, the fifth settler in our county, being preceded only by Elias Hughes, John Ratliff, Benjamin Green and Richard Pitzer.

ISAAC and JOHN STADDEN.

1800.

Isaac Stadden, Esq., and Colonel John Stadden were pioneer settlers in the Licking valley of the year 1800. They came from Northumberland county, Pennsylvania. John was a widower, and had been in the service of some government surveying party, which was probably the means of bringing to his notice the beautiful valley of the Licking. It was probably the same party to which he was attached as ax-man or chain-carrier, that Captain Elias Hughes served as a hunter. Isaac Stadden had a wife and two children, and was living in the county of Northumberland, Pennsylvania.

In the spring of 1800 these veteran pioneers came up the Licking valley and entered upon some bottom land, partially cleared, a mile below Newark, now on the Jones farm, and built a hut or cabin. They soon prepared the ground and put in a crop. At the same time the Elliott's were raising corn below them, on the Davis farm, and Green and Pitzer were doing the same thing on Shawnee run, on the O'Banon farm, while near the mouth of "Bowling Green run" Hughes and Ratliff were similarly employed. And that was all the farming that was done on the Licking bottoms in the year 1800 between the junction of the North and South Forks of Licking and the present line of Muskingum county. The pioneers in the sparsely settled regions of the Northwest Territory, in those days, were not favored abundantly with mail facilities, and no communications passed between Mr. Stadden and his wife during all those weary months that he was engaged in building a cabin, clearing land and raising corn, from early spring until late in the summer of the year 1800. This fact Mrs. Stadden

communicated to me herself. Great irregularities then attended the carrying of mails in the "far West." A mail was occasionally brought to Zanesville, then the nearest post office to the settlers in the upper valley of the Licking, but little reliance was placed upon it. If letters came through at all from the old settlements, the pioneers were lucky, even if they were a long time on the way, and were subject to high postage, about eight times our present rates.

In September, 1800, Mr. Isaac Stadden removed his family from Pennsylvania into the cabin erected for them in the spring. His was the second wagon that came up the Licking valley. Meanwhile, John Stadden, having made the acquaintance of Betsey Green, daughter of Benjamin, became enamored of the fair maid of Shawnee run, and after an honest courtship of reasonable length for pioneer times, she, nothing loth, having fallen into his notions on the subject, they resolved upon matrimony, and matrimony they committed, and it was the first offense of the kind in civilized life, within the present limits of Licking county! This pioneer marriage was to take place on the 10th of December, 1800, but it was not consummated until Christmas of that year. There was not a preacher or squire nearer than Zanesville, and when the late Judge Henry Smith, who was then an acting magistrate of the Northwest Territory, living at the mouth of Licking, was invited to perform the marriage ceremony in this case, on the 10th of December, he informed John that the territorial laws required that written notice of the intention of the parties be posted up at three conspicuous places for fifteen days before the wedding, and if that had been done he would be there. John's ignorance of territorial law suddenly brought him to anchor. He thereupon came home, stuck up the notices quick, and submitted as well as he could to the postponement of his happiness for the prescribed period of fifteen days

—hence the marriage on Christmas, instead of December 10th. Mrs. Isaac Stadden is good authority for the assertion that those fifteen days were a period of gloom, disappointment, despondency and discontent to at least the male member of the high contracting parties. Squire Smith came up the Licking on Christmas, and said the words which made John and Betsey one. A child born to them in the latter half of the year 1801, was the second birth in what is now Licking county, and its decease before the close of said year was the first death.

Mrs. Isaac Stadden related to me that late in October, 1800, her husband went into Cherry Valley to hunt deer, that being better hunting ground than the Licking Valley, and that he came home in the evening, greatly excited, having discovered the "Old Fort," of which he had not heard before. Next morning they mounted their horses and took a good look at this great curiosity, riding all around it on the top of the embankment. And so far as is known they were the first white persons who saw this great work of antiquity!

During the early years of the Stadden's residence here Indians were more or less numerous hereabouts, but they were pacifically disposed. Mrs. Stadden once gave me a humorous account of the attempt of a rather prominent one, who frequently came along, to buy her of her husband by the offer of a considerable number of skins of wild animals. The offer was made in good faith and somewhat pressed, but Mr. Stadden was not much in the trafficking mood on that occasion.

Another incident. In November, or early in December, 1800, Mr. Isaac Stadden went to hunt deer above the "Old Fort," near Ramp creek. There, towards evening, around a camp-fire, in the dense forest, he met John Jones, Phineas Ford, Frederick Ford, Benoni Benjamin and a Mr. Deuner. Jones and the Fords were married to the

sisters of Benjamin. Jones was of Welsh extraction, born in New Jersey, but had lived in the same neighborhood with Mr. Stadden in Pennsylvania, where they had been schoolmates. Neither knew that the other was in the Northwest Territory. Neither had seen the other for many years, and had known nothing of their intervening historics—their adventures, or of their whereabouts. The romantic interest of such a meeting, under such circumstances, can be better imagined by you than described by me. The Fords were Yankees, and Benjamin was a Pennsylvanian, and all became prominent pioneer settlers. When met at their camp fire by Stadden they were exploring with a view to settlement, and did settle in a very few months afterwards—Mr. Jones on the Munson farm, and the Fords and Benjamin on Ramp creek. Denner became a day laborer for McCauly, who located near the mouth of Ramp creek early in 1801. The company accepted Mr. Stadden's invitation to visit him at his cabin, and did so, soon, and all hands hugely enjoyed that visit. Jones raised a crop of corn in the Licking bottoms near Stadden's cabin in the summer of 1801.

John Stadden moved to "Hog run" in 1802, and in 1808 was elected sheriff (the first one) of Licking county, in which office he served two years. He was also for some years collector of taxes, and held other positions of honor and trust in military and civil life. His son, Richard, was sheriff of this county from 1834 to 1838, and was, in the last named year, elected a member of the Senate of Ohio.

Colonel John Stadden was a man of integrity, uprightness, and a fair degree of intelligence. Late in life he removed with his wife to Illinois, where they died. They were honored and highly esteemed while living, and died leaving a reputation untarnished. He and his wife were original members of the first Methodist society formed in this county, which was in 1804, by Rev. Asa Shinn.

Mr. Isaac Stadden was a carpenter by trade, and brought with him a sett of carpenter's tools, which he used to the great convenience of the neighborhood. Especially was he useful in the making of all the coffins needed by the early settlers for a number of years. The coffin for Mrs. Ratliff, who died in 1802, was made by him, and so were many others. They were at first made out of puncheons split out, and then hewed and planed off.

Mr. Isaac Stadden built a "handmill" during the winter after he came for the purpose of grinding the corn grists of his few neighbors, as well as for his own accommodation. And this was the first essay at millbuilding within the limits of our county, with the possible exception of one, a "make-shift," previously got up by Elias Hughes. He raised a crop on the same ground in 1801, and in the spring of 1802 he moved upon land he purchased two miles farther down the valley, upon which he lived until his death in 1841, and upon which Mrs. Stadden lived until her death, which took place July 3d, 1870, a period of sixty-eight years. She reached the ripe age of ninety years.

In 1801 the township of Licking, in Fairfield county, was organized Its southern boundary was the north line of the "Refugee lands;" its northern boundary was the north line of the United States Military Lands; and its eastern and western boundaries were the then eastern and western boundaries of the county of Fairfield, and included almost the entire territory of the present counties of Licking and Knox. To complete the organization of the township an election was held at the cabin of Elias Hughes, on the first day of January, 1802, and Isaac Stadden was elected Justice of the Peace. I believe Mr. James Maxwell was elected constable. In a year or two John Warden was elected the successor of Mr. Stadden. He served a short time and resigned, and William Wright in 1804, or a little later, succeeded to

the office. He resided in Newark.

Great difficulties were encountered by the early settlers in procuring fruit trees. It is true that the very eccentric character known as "Johnny Appleseed" had started many nurseries west of the Ohio river, some of them even before our State was organized, but in consequence of his neglect of them they never came to be of much practical utility. "Johnny" was not a practical man, but he meant well. Only one nursery was started by him within the present limits of our county, and that was on what is known as the "Scotland farm," about three miles in a northeasterly direction from Newark. It was neglected, and left unenclosed, so that domestic animals browsed upon it, and it afforded but few, if any, trees for transplanting.

A short time after Isaac Stadden moved upon his own land he formed a partnership with a man for the purpose of starting a nursery of fruit trees. They accordingly cleared about two acres of ground and dedicated it to that purpose. It succeeded admirably and in about three years they commenced the sale of fruit trees, and that nursery furnished the beginnings of the orchards of numerous pioneers in this section of the State. And pecuniarily it was a success also. A writer in the last November number of *Harpers Monthly* says that "Johnny Appleseed" was Isaac Stadden's partner in this nursery, which is a great mistake. A much more practical man by the name of "Johnny Goldthwaite" was his partner. He was an experienced horticulturist, and removing to Fairfield county he there supplied, for many years, an extensive section of country with fruit trees from his nursery. These facts came to me from Mrs. Stadden's own lips, and are, therefore, reliable. She knew both Johnny's well. And here I might add that Mrs. Stadden took up and placed in her chest three very small apple trees, on leaving her home in Pennsylvania, in 1800, for

the West, and planted them with her own hands, and again in 1802 removed them to their own farm. One of those trees, although it is over seventy years since the last transplanting, is still living and bearing fruit.

Of the two children brought by Mr. and Mrs. Stadden to the Licking valley in the year 1800 . only one, (Margaret) survives. She married a Mr. Gillin, and is now living in Nebraska. A number of children were born to them after their arrival. Several have died, and among those still living are Mrs. Melissa Wright, of Kirtland, Ohio, who was born in 1802; Mrs. McCrum, of Columbus, Ohio; Sarah Fleming and Catharine Jones, of Tuscola, Illinois. Three sons (Elijah, Henry and Mathias) live in Licking county. Catharine is married to a son of the John Jones whom Mr. Stadden found at the camp-fire in Cherry Valley late in the year 1800, of which mention has been made.

Isaac Stadden was a man of retiring habits, unostentatious, religiously disposed, given to acts of neighborly kindness, and practiced, to a liberal extent, the virtues that characterized our pioneer fathers. He never felt the degrading meanness of avarice, but he made ample provision for the comfort of those of his surviving family, who were unable to provide for themselves. His estimable widow, who so long survived him, had a home and all its comforts to the close of her long life.

Mrs. Stadden's ancestors (the Kleiber's) were of German origin. She was born in 1780, in Pennsylvania, just before the close of the revolutionary war. She, when eighteen years of age, entered into the married relation, and two years afterwards came to the Licking valley. She was one of our model pioneer women, and it may be truly asserted that she always, throughout her long career, discharged with rare fidelity, the obligations that devolved upon her as wife and mother, and in all the relations of

life. She had a most wonderful memory. Our society obtained more facts from her in relation to early-time history than from any other person, and rare accuracy uniformly characterized her statements. She was not less distinguished for devotion to truth than for her remarkable memory, especially of her accurate recollection of events that transpired in the early part of her life. She had a good intellect, sound judgment and excellent sense; her seventy years of active life and large experience among us could not fail, therefore, superadded to her fine qualities of heart, and her high sense of moral obligations to make her rank with the best class of our pioneer women. She was a woman of rare frankness and candor —of great integrity of character and fidelity to her convictions. She heartily cherished the Christian faith during the last sixty years of her life, practically responding to its requirements with her characteristic fidelity. Living without reproach she was as honored in death as esteemed during her long life. In the evening of her life it was light all about her.

CAPTAIN SAMUEL ELLIOTT.

1800.

"God bless the noble Pioneers,
Their names on history's page will live—
Their virtue shall survive in song;
Honor and praise to them belong."

Captain Samuel Elliott located in the valley of the Licking, one and a half miles below the junction of the North and South Forks, now Newark, in September, 1800. In the spring of this year he, with two sons, left his mountain home in Allegheny county, Maryland, and came to this valley where they erected a cabin and planted corn and potatoes, and then returned home for the family. This cabin was built near the big spring on the farm now owned by T. J. Davis, Esq. He may have been drawn to this point in order to be neighbor to the Messrs. Green and Pitzer, who had just located on Shawnee run, about half a mile eastward, on the O'Banon farm. They all came from the same neighborhood in Maryland. In the autumn Captain Elliott, with his wife and twelve children, arrived and took possession of his cabin and harvested his crops. He made the seventh family that located in what is now Licking county. Isaac Stadden, with his family, preceded him a few days, who located on what is now the Jones farm. The families of Hughes, Ratliff, Green, Pitzer, Van Buskirk, Stadden and Elliott were all that lived in the Licking valley until the Christmas of 1800, when the marriage of John Stadden and Betsey Green constituted another, making the eighth family in our county, which comprised the entire population at the close of the year 1800.

While Captain Elliott lived here he entertained for several days Rev. McDonald, a missionary of the Presbyterian Church, who preached the first sermon ever delivered within the limits of Licking county. It was late in 1801 or early in 1802.

The manufacture of a web of twenty yards of nettle cloth or linen by the wife and daughters of Captain Elliott, while they resided here, was one of the novel events of the day. In the absence of flax it was the best they could do. Such were the expedients necessity compelled pioneers to resort to.

Captain Elliott was born near Ballymena, County Antrim, Province of Ulster, in Ireland, in 1751. On coming to North America, in 1771, he settled in the colony of

Pennsylvania, near Philadelphia. Here he lived during the dawning era of the Revolution, and when that great struggle for human freedom was fully inaugurated he took sides with the oppressed colonists—the champions of self-government. Towards the close of the revolutionary war Captain Elliott married in Northampton county, Pennsylvania, from where he emigrated to western Maryland, settling west of Cumberland, in Allegheny county. Here he remained until his removal to the Licking valley in the year 1800.

Captain Elliott built the first hewed log house erected in Newark, which was in 1802. It stood on the lot of Mrs. Fullerton, on East Main street. He moved into it during the same year, which made him one of Newark's earliest inhabitants. He soon purchased of General Schenck, one of the proprietors of Newark, some lands lying about a mile west of the village, upon which he settled in 1804, and where he remained until his death, which occurred May 24th, 1831. The death of Mrs. Elliott took place on the same farm, May 19th, 1822, aged sixty-four years. She was a woman of rare excellency of character; of model characteristics as a housewife; neighborly, accommodating, kind, industrious, charitable; raised her children respectably; ruled her household well; taught industry and the virtues to her children by precept and example, hence, it is not surprising that her daughters became good women, and her sons useful men. She died in communion with the Presbyterian Church in Newark, and her pastor, Rev. S. S. Miles, who is still living and a citizen of Illinois, commemorated her virtues in an appreciative but discriminative obituary sketch of her, published in the Newark *Advocate* of May 23d, 1822, *over fifty years ago*, then conducted by the late Mr. Benjamin Briggs. Mrs. Elliott lived a life of devotion to the interests of her husband, her children, and the church. Though dead, in friendship's silent register she lives—a numerous posterity revere her memory.

Upon the organization of Licking county in 1808, Captain Elliott became the Coroner, and served many years in that office, and was succeeded therein by his son, Alexander, who also served many years.

Captain Samuel Elliott was Providentially preserved until he completed the eightieth year of his age before he was summoned to his better inheritance. His death occurred in May, 1831, and the obituary notice of him appears in the Newark *Advocate* of date May 26, 1831, written by the then editor, Mr. Briggs.

Captain Elliott, as well as Mrs. Elliott, and indeed most if not all of their children, adopted the Presbyterian form of faith, and were upright, industrious, frugal, highly esteemed and faithful in all the relations of life. But few, if any, of our early-time settlers more generally practiced the pioneer virtues.

Fidelity, integrity, candor, veracity, sincerity, frankness, were the leading characteristics of the venerable Elliott, the honored pioneer of the Licking valley. I knew the patriarchal, gray-haired patriot well, and it affords me more than ordinary pleasure to be able, though more than forty years have elapsed since his death, to bear testimony to his many virtues, and to make mention of his useful life and honorable career. "Peace to the just man's memory—let it grow greener with years, and blossom in the flight of ages."

The venerable Elliott, I have indicated, participated actively in our Revolution. He was patriotic to the core, and remained so to the close of his useful, honored, octogenarian career. And it may also be said that patriotism came to be a characteristic of his descendants. Three of the sons of Captain Elliott were personally engaged in the war of 1812, and another, at the same time, patriotically sent a substitute, as he

was unable by reason of feeble health to do soldier's duty himself. Our esteemed patriot's grandsons, David Taylor and Alexander Elliott, served with honor in the Mexican war, and two grandsons, William and Jonathan Taylor, brothers of David, served long and faithfully in the Union army during the late rebellion. William encountered a rebel's fatal bullet in the gallant and successful attack upon the enemy's works at Arkansas Post—Jonathan survived "the march to the sea" with Sherman's army. Reuben Lonceford, and a number of other great-grandsons, also fought the rebels, including two young Elliotts, who, as Union soldiers, lost their lives during the great rebellion. Lieutenant Reuben Harris, a grandson, was long a gallant officer in our Navy, and died in the service.

One of the older sons of the veteran Elliott never came to the Licking valley. When the family came he was absent in the Mississippi Territory, and had been sick, but was thought to be convalescent. As he was never afterwards heard from, it was thought by the family that he relapsed and died. At all events all subsequent efforts to obtain letters from him proved abortive. The other twelve children were all in subsequent life identified with the Licking valley. A number of them died in early life. Most that survived until they approached middle life, married, Nancy, who died October 28th, 1871, in Newark, was the exception.

One of the daughters became the wife of Mr. James Gill, an early settler of Newark. Another intermarried with Dr. Noah Harris, who came to Newark to practice his profession about the year 1808, and had a successful professional career of nearly twenty-five years here. He left quite a number of children who were well educated by their mother, and all became respectable members of the community. Mrs. Harris was a woman of great energy of character, and otherwise well qualified to discharge the great responsibilities of her position. She lived to see her children enter manhood and womanhood, but most of them died early—only two survive.

Mrs. Harris displayed great heroism in meeting adverse fortune and afflictive dispensations of Providence. She also possessed in an eminent degree those social and domestic virtues that so distinguished our pioneer mothers.

Mrs. Harris died near Newark, August 16th, 1863, at the age of seventy-three years, greatly esteemed by her relations and acquaintances.

The late Hon. Horatio J. Harris was a son of Dr. Harris, and a grandson of the pioneer Captain Elliott. He attained to high position in public life, and may be regarded as a successful politician, who was not without a good share of ability. He was a native of Newark, but removed in early life to Indiana, where he served respectively in the offices of Clerk of the Senate, State Senator and Auditor of State. During General Taylor's presidential term he was appointed District Attorney of Mississippi, having previously moved to that State. Ill health soon compelled him to resign his office. He came to Newark on a visit to his relatives, where he died, having scarcely reached middle life. He was a young man of much promise, and would, undoubtedly, have reached higher positions and greater distinction had his life and health been preserved.

Sarah was the youngest of those twelve children brought by her father, Captain Samuel Elliott, to the Licking valley in 1800. She was born in Allegheny county, Maryland, May 2nd, 1798, and died in Newark, May 13th, 1872, aged seventy-four years. Sarah Elliott and the late General Jonathan Taylor were married in 1821, and lived happily in said relation until April, 1848, when he died—died near "the noon of life"—when he had just passed the meridian of his manhood

and had just attained to the full maturity of his intellectual powers. Warm in his friendships, kind, affable in his intercourse with mankind, hospitable, companionable, cheerful in temperament, exemplary in all the relations of life, he could not fail to have many friends who greatly deplored his death. He is remembered by many of us as our Representative in both branches of the General Assembly, and as a member, elected in 1838, of the Congress of the United States. He long enjoyed the respect, and commanded the confidence of his many friends and acquaintances.

In the relations of husband, father, friend, he met the requisitions made upon him to a generous, an unusual extent, and many that survived him had abundant reasons to cherish sunny memories of him—to think kindly of him now, and

"In the far years to come."

General Taylor led a very active life and was a commanding character in the community. He attracted to him, and brought under his personal influence very many young men—gave direction to their views—moulded their opinions, and exerted a controlling influence in forming their habits—in establishing their characters—shaping their destinies. Although zealously devoted to politics for twenty years, it is an act of simple justice to his memory to say that he scrupulously shunned the politicians vices, and uniformly cast the weight of his influence, preceptively and practically, on the side of good order, sound morality, temperance and religion.

At the time of General Taylor's death his oldest son, David, was a soldier in Mexico. He was a youth of genuine manhood and was greatly relied upon to take his father's place in the conduct of the business affairs of the family, and came home to do so, but also died in a few months after his return, leaving his widowed mother with but three sons, and they all in early childhood. One of those went down amidst the clash of contending armies on the battle-field during the great rebellion. Another is a citizen of the West; and only one (Waldo) remains among us. He is known to most of us as a rising, ambitious young lawyer of fair promise and talents, whose energy, go-a-head-a-tiveness, enterprise, industry and good qualities of head and heart will entitle him to, and will doubtless secure to him a good measure of success.

Mrs. Taylor was one of the excellent of the earth—a model pioneer woman, who practiced all the matronly virtues, led an industrious, useful life, and died regretted by many friends. She had a fine intellect, sound judgment, good sense, and had, by observation, intercourse with the world, and also by reading acquired a large fund of information. Mrs. Taylor always cherished the Christian faith, and had been for more than forty years in communion with the Presbyterian Church. Living, during her childhood and early womanhood among the frontier settlers, and being left in widowhood in charge of a large family, twenty-four years ago, many requisitions were, of course, made upon her for the exhibition of the qualities above ascribed to her, and for the practice of the high womanly virtues which distinguished her honored and preeminently useful career of seventy-four years.

Mrs. Taylor, in the order of Providence was called to encounter more of the ills incident to humanity than fell to the lot of most persons, and to grapple with an unusual allotment of the sterner realities of life, but she met them with firmness, composure, resignation, and with more than the lauded heroism of Roman matrons—with the overcoming energy and stout-heartedness of a western pioneer woman—with the fortitude of a Christian mother, whose life was one of faith, and love, patience and devotion to her family. And how much of faith, love, patience, courage and devotion to her fatherless ones she exhibited

in kindness, amiability, affection, during those long years of her widowhood, few can know.

The writer's acquaintance with Mrs. Taylor dates back to the period of her early womanhood, soon after she had entered into the marriage relation, and continued uninterrupted for almost half a century, during the maturity of her life, and through the years of her serene old age, which she gradually, beautifully, brought to a close in the conscientious performance of every duty, and the discharge of all her obligations.

Mrs. Taylor leaves four surviving children, two of whom reside in the West, and two (Mrs. C. T. Dickinson and her son Waldo) in Newark. Four of her children died after reaching maturity. It is gratifying to know that all her living children were present during her last protracted illness.

Mrs. Taylor's funeral obsequies were conducted by the Rev. H. M. Hervey, Wednesday, May 15th. when a large circle of surviving friends accompanied her to their last resting place in Cedar Hill Cemetery.

Thus went down to the tomb this venerable and highly esteemed matron of our early days, after a well spent life of so many years. peacefully, happily, the anguish of parting in the dying hour, with children and surviving friends, being relieved by blissful memories of the Past, and by joyful hopes of the Future, cheered by the beautiful faith that to her

"This life was but a suburb of the life elysian."

OUR PIONEERS OF 1801.

John Larabee was one of the veteran pioneers of the Licking valley of the year 1801, which was seven years before the county of Licking was organized. Mr. Larabee was born in Lynn, Massachusetts, in 1760, and was of English descent, his ancestors having emigrated at an early period from Great Britain, and settled in New England. His father led a seafaring life, and is supposed to have been impressed into the British service, from which he never returned. His son, John, the subject of this sketch, came under the guardianship of one of his uncles, with whom he lived until he was fifteen years of age. At this time hostilities were commenced by the mother country against her colonies, and John Larabee being unable to get his uncle's consent to go soldiering took "French leave" of him and identified himself with our revolutionary struggle for Independence from its very commencement. John's guardian, he alleged. worked him very hard and gave him no education whatever, which was certainly true as to the last charge. for Mr. Larabee never learned even to read. Leading so hard a life at his uncle's, John was in a great measure justifiable for taking the course he did. He first entered the service as a waggoner, in which capacity he served his country for two years with fidelity and acceptability. He then volunteered as a common soldier, a private, and carried the musket, faithfully discharging his duty to the end of that great struggle. He, of course, during five years active service as a soldier, was in many engagements. but on this point I have been unable to obtain much reliable or authentic information, except the fact that he participated in the capture of the Hessians at Trenton, and on that occasion

badly froze his feet. That he was a good soldier and gallantly bore himself throughout the war is established by the fact that he received an honorable discharge at the close of that sanguinary struggle. During many of the latter years of his life he regularly received a pension, which was a grateful recognition of the inestimable services of this brave hero of the revolution. A benificent government could not do less—a grateful people would have sanctioned even much more.

It does not appear that Mr. Larabee ever returned again to his uncle's. A seven year's absence had alienated him from his old attachments, and having so little respect for his uncle, it is not remarkable that he should be indifferent towards him. But *where* he lived, or *how* he employed himself during the twenty years that immediately succeeded the revolution I have been unable to learn. But there is a strong probability that soon after the close of the revolutionary war he came to the western frontiers and was employed in some capacity against the Indians. It is also probable that he was in the expeditions of Harmar, St. Clair and Wayne, and perhaps in others. All this is rendered the more probable from the fact that when we again get authentic knowledge of him he was at or near Marietta, probably on the Virginia side of the Ohio river. This was in the year 1800, when he was a married man and the father of a child or two.

In the spring of 1801, Mr. Larabee, leaving his family behind, embarked with others in a canoe, for the rich bottoms of the Licking, carrying some bacon and other supplies with them for a partial subsistence during the summer. A portion of his fellow-emigrants came by land, driving the stock, of which Mr. Larabee owned a yoke of oxen and two cows—the latter were to contribute to his subsistence, and the former were to be made useful in the clearing of the land, the building of a cabin, and the raising of a crop of corn. He came up the Muskingum and Licking rivers in his canoe and landed on the south side of the latter stream, nearly opposite the mouth of the Bowling Green Run, and squatted on land now owned by William O'Banon. Here he found a hollow sycamore tree in which he domiciled for the next few months. It furnished him a room of more than ten feet in diameter, and was amply capacious for all his purposes. He cleared the land and raised a few acres of corn, and also at his leisure during the summer built himself a cabin. The Larabee colony, by the time they reached the Bowling Green, including all that came by land and water, having received some accessions by the way, numbered some eleven persons. One of these was James Maxwell, the first school teacher that came to our county—he was also our first constable. He was also a great song-singer. It was said that he knew and could sing a song for every day in the year. Some of his descendants abide with us to the present day.

Mr. Larabee's habitation (a hollow tree) was the most primitive sort. The hut, built of small logs, or rather poles, such as two men could lay up, was the second in the upper grade of habitations. The cabin built of much larger logs was the third style. These were covered with clabboards. The hewed log house covered with shingles was next in order. This was followed by the frame building similarly covered. Lastly we have the brick and stone houses. These are the style at present. Larabee's style in the hollow tree contrasts amazingly with that of one of our modern brick mansions and proves the seventy-one intervening years to have been steadily marked by progress—most wonderful progress! All these habitation dispensations have been witnessed by many still living!

Having built a cabin and raised a crop of corn, Mr. Larabee returned for his family, and in the autumn of

1801 brought them up from Marietta to their new home, where they lived a pioneer life for a number of years. Being prospered somewhat, he bought a tract of land of Judge Smith and Thomas Seymour, situated a mile or two southwest from his hollow sycamore on which he settled for life.

As already stated, Mr. Larabee was wholly illiterate. He was unpretentious, honest, industrious, and measurably free from the degrading vices and vicious habits that sometime characterized the frontier settlers. And it can also be truthfully said that he practiced the virtues which so conspicuously marked the character of our pioneers, and, indeed of most of the settlers of a new country—virtues which grew out of the necessities of their condition, foremost of which were industry, frugality and hospitality, and last and most general, the reciprocation of neighborly kindnesses. In his childhood Mr. Larabee was under Quaker influences, but during the last twenty-five or thirty years of his life he was a member of the Disciples' Church, and sustained a fair Christian character. He died February 6th, 1846, aged fourscore and six years.

A prominent fact in the career and history of John Larabee is that he entered the service of his country at the *beginning*, and remained in it to the *close* of the revolutionary war! Of how few, comparatively, of the soldiers of the revolution could this be said. But of John Larabee *it can be said* that he was in the service of his country during the whole period of our revolutionary struggle. *Forever honored be such patriot soldiers!*

Another prominent fact in the career and history of John is that he ascended the Licking river in a canoe as early as 1801, and lived in a hollow tree for months, while preparing a home for his family, and raising a crop for their subsistence, enduring meanwhile, to a large extent, the dangers, privations and hardships incident to frontier life.

All honor to the memory of such Pioneers!

Mr. James Maxwell was of those who came with John Larabee. He was distinguished as a singer of songs—was elected constable (our first) in January, 1802, of Licking township, Fairfield county, and devoted himself to school teaching for many years. He married a daughter of Eliss Hughes—has long since deceased, but some of his descendants remain. Mr. John Weedman, whose history has been given, was another of the Larabee colony. So probably, also, was a Mr. Carpenter, who squatted near to or on the Bowling Green. Samuel Parr settled on the Licking bottoms just below the junction of the North and South Forks. James McCauley and James Danner located near the mouth of Ramp creek, where the former built a "tub-mill" or "corn-cracker," the first water power concern built in the county. Phillip Barrick settled near the Licking Narrows. He was a Jerseyman who came to the Licking valley in 1793, and lived near where the Claypool Mills now are, until the spring of 1801 (some accounts say until 1802) when he removed six or eight miles farther up the valley, near the Licking Narrows. He was a man of energy, industry, enterprise and influence, conducting successfully his farm, together with a tavern and a distillery.

It was in the spring of this year also when Phineas and Frederick Ford and Benoni Benjamin came over from the Sciota and settled near the line of Newark and Union townships, now Union Station, which also made them the neighbors of Mr. John Van Buskirk, and of McCauley and Danner. Mr. John Jones, who came over from the Sciota with them, settled in the Raccoon valley, on the Munson farm, and there built the first cabin erected within the limits of Granville township. He was brother-in-law of the Fords and Benjamin. These gentlemen are

thought by some to have settled here a year earlier, but the weight of evidence is against that idea. They were here, however, as explorers, during the year 1800, for, as already stated, they spent a night around a camp-fire near Ramp creek, in company with Isaac Stadden, late in November or early in December of that year.

Phillip Sutton, Job Rathbone and John and George Gillespie, the two former Pennsylvanians, and perhaps the latter also, settled on Hog run, in Licking township, and were the pioneer settlers there. The Gillespies became land owners, but soon sold out. In November, 1801, they sold fifty acres to Phillip Sutton, and in February, 1802, one hundred and fifty acres to Benjamin Green, which closed out their stock of land, and they remained but a short time after selling out. Job Rathbone was a brother-in-law of Jehu Sutton, one of the oldest, earliest and best known pioneers of Licking township, who died a few years since, leaving a widow who is now well along in her ninety-sixth year.

John Edwards came to the South Fork valley and settled on Van Buskirk's land in September, 1801. They had been neighbors and friends in Brooke county, Virginia. He was distinguished as a hunter and as an expert with the rifle, having been engaged as a spy for some years on the frontiers of Virginia as well as in the Northwest Territory. He was a man of energy, industry and great force of character. He was moved by Mr. George Wells, a neighbor, Edwards going before, blazing the trees and killing game, while those with the wagon cut out the road where necessary.

The above is probably a full, or at least a *nearly* complete list of our pioneers who came during the year 1801. They were, for the most part, men of enterprise, daring, courage, industry, cleverness, hospitality, and generally practiced the virtues and fell into the vices that characterized the pioneers of the Northwest Territory.

Late in the year General W. C. Schenck, father of General Robert C. Schenck, arrived, took boarding with Isaac Stadden, and arranged the preliminaries during the winter of 1801-2 for laying out the town of Newark in the spring which was accordingly done.

For more extended biographical sketches of a number of the foregoing pioneers of 1801, the reader is referred to Dr. Wilson's Pioneer Paper, No. 17; to Captain M. M. Munson's paper, No. 14; to Pioneer Pamphlet, No. 5, by Samuel Park, Esq., and to Pioneer Papers Nos. 19, 47, 86 and others, by the writer hereof.

OUR PIONEERS OF 1802.

The year 1802 brought us many new settlers The accessions were large, much in excess of the previous year, and a number of them were men of some means, and of more than ordinary consideration, influence and intelligence. Of this class were Alexander Holmes, Theophilus Rees, Jacob Nelson, Abraham Wright and others.

Alexander Holmes was a brother-in-law of John Van Buskirk and James Hendricks, and all three removed from Brooke county, Virginia, to the valley of the South Fork Holmes and Hendricks came in 1802 and settled upon portions of the Van Buskirk tract.

Alexander Holmes was a surveyor, and assisted in the surveys of much of the public lands in the north-western portion of Ohio for the general government. He also surveyed much land in Licking county, and also was surveyor in the location of many of our roads in early times. We are also indebted to him for the first complete survey of the ancient works in the vicinity of Newark.

Alexander Holmes, upon the organization of the judiciary of Licking county in 1808, became one of the three Associate Judges of the Court of Common Pleas, which position he held until 1812. He was again elected Judge in 1823, and served until 1828. As a Judge he was upright, intelligent, incorruptible. His independence and ability were sometimes manifested in the delivery of dissenting opinions, when he entertained views on points in issue different from those of the President Judge.

Judge Holmes was a gentleman of considerable natural ability—of general intelligence and extensive information—and was of the better educated class of our pioneers. He led an active, useful, industrious life. Few men were more intimately connected with the early settlement and early history of our county than Judge Holmes, or manifested a greater degree of interest in its prosperity, or who more readily and actively espoused measures that were calculated to promote the public welfare, socially, intellectually and morally.

A more extended notice of Judge Holmes can be found in Pioneer Papers Nos. 19 and 36.

James Hendricks, just before leaving Brooke county, Virginia, married the daughter of Mr. William Murphy, a distinguished pioneer, Rev. Dr. Joseph Doddridge, the historian of Western Pennsylvania and Virginia, being the officiating clergyman. He brought his bride to the home he had purchased, being part of the Buskirk tract, where he lived for a number of years, and where our esteemed friend, Mr. Benjamin Hendricks, of the vicinity of Newark, was born to them, on New Year's day, 1803, which makes him now the oldest native male citizen residing in our county. After a few years Mr. Hendricks sold out and purchased a farm near Newark upon which he lived until his death in 1855. Mrs. Hendricks survived him a number of years, having reached a good old age. She, as well as her sisters, the wives of Judge Holmes and John Van Buskirk, was intelligent, highly esteemed, and well adapted to life on the frontiers.

Mr. Hendricks was an inoffensive, industrious, unambitious, unpretending, honest man, a good citizen, who led a quiet, peaceable, virtuous life, and died esteemed by all who knew him.

Theophilus Rees came to Pennsylvania from Carmarthenshire, South Wales, in 1795. Having purchased, in company with Thomas Phillips, a large tract of land on the Welsh Hills, he removed from Beulah, Cambria county, Pennsylvania, upon it in 1802. David Lewis and David Thomas, his sons in-law, accompanied him, as did also James Johnson and Simon James, which makes all of them pioneers of 1802.

Mr. Theophilus Rees was a man of means, of great integrity of character, of commanding influence, of elevated moral tone, of some scholarship, and was of great usefulness to his countrymen settled about him. He was mainly instrumental in the organization of the Welsh Hills Baptist Church in 1808. Mr. Rees died in 1813.

An elaborate biographical sketch of Mr. Rees will be found in Pioneer Pamphlet No. 2; also in Pioneer Paper No. 41. Pioneer Papers Nos. 14 and 42 have some notice of him also.

Jacob Nelson, being the owner of a large tract of land in the Licking valley, settled upon it, a mile and a half below Newark. After a few years he built a mill and then sold

out. John Warden, Abraham Miller and Henry Claybaugh, (the two last mentioned being brothers in law,) came from the South Branch of the Potomac, and went into the improvement of their lands east of and near Newark. They bought of General Schenck, their deeds bearing date May 20th, 1802, the contracts had probably been made weeks before. John Warden, in 1803, became the successor of Isaac Stadden in the office of Justice of the Peace, the latter having resigned it. Abraham Miller raised a crop and returned to the South Branch in the autumn of 1802, where he married, and in the spring of 1803 he brought his wife and became a permanent settler on the first farm east of Newark, John Warden owning and occupying the second one.

Michael Thorn, Frederick Myers and Henry Neff located at or near the Little Bowling Green, about a mile south of Linnville, in Bowling Green township. They came from the Monongahela country in Western Virginia.

Adam Hatfield, James Black and Richard Parr settled in Newark this year, Black locating himself on the St. Nicholas house lot, in the capacity of a "tavern keeper." Seven houses were built in Newark during 1802, the other four being built and occupied by Samuel Elliott. Henry Claybaugh, Samuel Parr and Samuel Elliott, Jr., who, except Claybaugh, came before this year. The younger Elliott may have had a tenant in his house. Beall Babbs, Mrs. Catharine Pegg and James Jeffries settled in the vicinity of Newark during this year also.

Jonathan Benjamin, father-in-law of John Jones and the Ford brothers, located on Ramp creek in the spring of this year. He had passed through the French and Indian wars, and through the revolutionary war also, and had been a frontiersman from his youth up. He was regarded as a remarkable man in many respects. Mr. Benjamin was a man of good morals, industrious and honest, and religiously inclined. His life was one of extreme hardship, notwithstanding he lived to the extraordinary age of *one hundred and three years!* His married life continued with the wife of his youth almost four score years. He was born in 1738, and died in this county in 1841.

For a very interesting biographical sketch of this centenarian Ramp creek pioneer of 1802, the reader is referred to Mr. Samuel Parks' excellent pamphlet, being Pioneer Pamphlet No. 5, pages 19 and 20.

During this year the South Fork valley now Union township, had accessions in the persons of William and John Horned, James Green, Henry Owens, William Richardson, John Wagy and George, Richard, Joseph, Bazaleel and William Wells. This numerous Wells family came from Brooke county, Virginia.

Patrick Cunningham was born in Tyrone county, Province of Ulster, Ireland, and came to the Licking valley in 1802, settling near the cabin of John Jones, on the Munson farm. His was the second cabin built in the township. He lived here until 1803, or perhaps a little later, and then removed to Newark where he became quite a character. He was the father of John Cunningham, who was Sheriff, Auditor, and served many years as Justice of the Peace.

During the autumn of this year quite a little colony came from Washington county, Pennsylvania and settled in Newark and its vicinity. The men that composed it were William B. Gaw, Abraham Johnson James Petticord, Edward Nash Carlton, Benedict, Aquilla and two John Belts, and Abraham Wright. Abraham Johnson was long known as a tavern keeper in Newark. John Belt and James Petticord soon erected a mill at the east end of Newark, which, in a year or two they sold to John Van Buskirk. John Johnson, of Newark, is the only surviving son of Abraham Johnson, and has had a longer resi

dence here (70 years) than any person now living. In December, 1802, a daughter was born to Mr. Johnson, who is still living in Newark, and is the oldest native citizen. I believe she was the first child born here. She is the widow of Henry Haughey. Mrs. John Cunningham, born in 1803, is the next oldest native citizen of Newark.

Abraham Wright located in Newark and remained there until 1806, when he removed up the North Fork eight miles, where, after a couple of years' residence, he located himself finally in the Clear Fork valley, on the borders of Newton and McKean townships, eight miles from Newark. His surviving son, Jacob Wright, Esq., whom he brought with him in 1802, and who is now one of our oldest settlers, is, I believe, the occupant of his father's old homestead.

Abraham Wright (printed by mistake of the writer, William Wright, in the paper on the Stadden's,) was a gentleman of ability, intelligence, and of excellent moral and religious character. He was a Methodist and gave hospitality to Revs. Asa Shinn, Peter Cartwright and James Quinn. The two last named preached sometimes at his house. On John Warden's resignation of the office of Justice of the Peace of Licking township, Fairfield county, in 1804, Abraham Wright succeeded to it and performed its duties, I believe, until his removal from town. One of his official acts, Captain Munson relates in Pioneer Paper No. 14, was the taking the acknowledgments of the seventy-eight proprietors or partners of the partition deed of the Granville company, on the 8th of March, 1806.

And this, I think, completes the list of Licking immigrants for the year 1802.

THE PIONEER WOMEN OF THE WEST.

BY REV. MRS. C. SPRINGER.

[*Read before the Licking County Pioneer Historical and Antiquarian Society, at their annual meeting held in the " Old Fort," near Newark, July 4th, 1872, and published by special request*]

The careful student of the Past, or the close observer of the Present cannot fail to be impressed with this fact: That God works out his divine purposes very frequently, not so much by great and overwhelming forces as by the over-ruling of what we are pleased to term insignificant events, to bring about and accomplish His grandest designs. It has been asserted by those who have given the subject their time and attention that when He has a great work to be done, and the time arrives for its accomplishment, that great minds are called specially into existence for its performance. It may be a question whether or not this is true. We are inclined to think times make men quite as often as men make times. For the abstruse discussion of this question, we have, however, neither time or inclination; the fact that directly concerns us is that when great things are to be done great minds have always been found to do them. It will be necessary for us in the treatment of the subject assigned us for to day, namely, "The character of the Pioneer Women of the West," not only to look backward in the study of their individual character, but to have at the same time constantly in mind the glorious golden Present, which we cannot truthfully deny is but the result of their patient work, the *product* of their heroic lives, the creation of their own genius. Being no less theirs because they toiled oft-times blindly for the supremely astounding results it was impossible for them to foresee. Before we enter into a personal examination of their character there is a point to which we wish to call your attention. It may at first seem foreign to our subject, but we assure you it is closely related to it. It is the growing inclination of the thinkers of to day to overestimate, yea, we may say to laud, magnify and worship genius, and to ignore and underrate what is ordinary. This very propensity has especially prejudiced us in our past opinions of the subject now before us. It was essentially necessary to the development of an uninhabited country that persons should move slowly, cautiously and considerately—this developed in individuals the very opposite of what constitutes in public opinion to day the necessary qualities to make men and women of mark and genius. We but prove our own obtuseness by failing to understand—or if you will allow a paradox—by forgetting to remember that "it is by the patient and diligent work at systematic adaptation to the eternal, by the rank and file of mankind, and the conscientious labor of each one in his little sphere of the

ture, whether psychical or physical, which in the necessary division of labor has fallen to his lot, that a condition of evolution is reached at which genius bursts forth." No one who gives attention can fail to discover how indispensable the humblest unit is in the social organism. It is profane for us to make the distinction we do when on this subject in regard to great and little things. It is imperatively necessary we should comprehend the great importance of the seemingly most common place occurrence in the formation of character, and to understand properly our subject we *must* consider this. We want all the evidence we can get subjectively, as well as objectively, in other words, what we can *feel* as well as *see*. We have before us as the aggregate work of the noble pioneers of the West what is to us indeed an incomprehensible result—incomprehensible not because it is more than we can believe, but because believing, it is more than we can comprehend. When the poet said "Westward the Star of Empire takes its way," there was, by inspiration, put into a single line of poetry the work of a century, and what required the intellects of several centuries successfully to develop. It is now no longer a misty myth or fabled story, given us through the inspiration of the poet, or as the dim vagaries of some brain steeped in the mythological lore of heathen ages. We care less to-day for the ideal than the real. We want more to know *what is*, than what might have been; and the results satisfy even the most painfully practical. This western world is a success. If it were even engulphed to-morrow it is no less a grand and glorious success, not only marking a new era in physical development, but having given birth to mind of the highest order—mind that will yet, in the presence of God, make an impression on eternity. Wipe out from existence this living west of the

Past and you wipe out the cause that gave, as its effect, voice to the lightning, wings to the wind, mind to matter; effect that the infinite Jehovah himself deigns to take in his hands for the accomplishment of his eternal purposes.

Shall we then, while viewing this massive structure, whose top outtops the highest mountain—shall we, because scaling its dizzy hights our gaze has been carried so far heavenward, forget the solid granite at its base, the underlying strata without which the entire superstructure must fall? This would, indeed, be the supremest of folly, reacting again the part of a heathen philosopher, who, while he gazed up at the stars, fell into the water. Bacon says had he looked down he might have seen the stars in the water, but looking up he could not see the water in the stars.

Our first plan was to present their character antithetically to contrast the pioneer women of the West with the average American women of to-day. But we confess when the light began to fall upon the canvas it pained our eyes and affected our consciousness. While it brought out strongly and strikingly the symmetry and grace of the one it exposed only the more painfully the incongruity and incompleteness of the other. We will have to acknowledge that we are wont to estimate ourselves as their superiors on account of the extreme acuteness of our sensitiveness, and the remarkable keenness of our perceptive faculties and our high appreciation of the Beautiful. That this may be true in regard to material subjects we readily admit; we are sad to say in regard to that higher and holier inner life which in herself and family woman has so much the power to develop, we are greatly their inferiors. We have too long regarded those women as plain, plodding matter-of-fact people with at least blunted sensibilities; let us rid our-

selves of all such mistaken ideas; the longer the world stands the more profoundly will be reverenced and respected their characters. It was the living of their quiet unobtrusive, yet most eventful lives, that gave birth to this American nation, and while they were, from the necessities of the case, practical and matter-of-fact, they were not by any means devoid of poetry or sentiment. Although books were scarce, and they had but little leisure, they were constantly in close communion with nature in all her moods, and unimpressible indeed must be the character, that can listen long unmoved to the intonations of her deep voiced inspirations. That their ears were not deaf to her teachings we conclude more from the character of their descendants than from the study of their own lives. The orators and poets directly descended from the Western pioneer women have won and occupied, deservedly, too, a niche in the temple of fame second to none, their characteristics being as decidedly their own as those of the more classical cast.

No women had a higher sense of honor, they were pre-eminently virtuous, retiring, and models of womanly modesty, humble, unobtrusive, yet courageous and immovable in the path of duty—plain and frugal, sparing of words, yet lavish of deeds.

We wish, for the sake of humanity, to get rid of the false ideas that delicateness of limb and attenuation of form are necessary to physical beauty, and that excitable imaginations and an entire indifference to the homely and common place constitute the spirituelle. The effect may not be so apparent on the present generation, but the unavoidable results will be a nation of imbeciles and idiots. It is no less a psychical than a physical truth that a healthy animal organism is necessary to perfect mental development, which is, indeed, impossible without it. It is strange, with all our boasted ad-

vance in the higher attainments, we have so long failed to see the intimate relation of mind and matter, and that ignoring this we cannot fail to suffer.

We have long been taught to admire the Roman and Spartan women. Their names have enlivened history's page and given birth to poetry from their own times until now; and as American women in whose veins still courses blood whose life-streams gave vitality and life to this Republic, we have had our own patriotism stirred and the innermost depths of ourselves roused by the example of their patriotism and disinterested sacrifice of self on the altar of their country, and yet when contrasted by the noble, disinterested, self-sacrificing, hardship-enduring character of our maternal progenitors of the West, we cannot but believe they will have to yield the palm. We always think of the former as we learned of them in times of war, roused by the invading foe, their republican blood at white heat; in their fury and excitement they seem akin to the gods; to us the very impersonation of energy and patriotism, and from their well-earned fame for heroism and valor we would not detract. Compared, however, with these matrons, the women of the West lose nothing. Having this distinctive trait they were earnest believers in and ardent supporters of the "Holy Christian Religion," to whose benign influences we are so largely indebted for our prosperity as a nation. It was those women who first implanted in the breast of the people Christian sentiments which gave us the desire for its blessed consolations. We admire the women of Sparta and Greece not less because we love the women of America. If it were possible for us to roll back "Old Time" for a century and live with them again the dark and dreary times of the first settlement of this country—when they literally walked by faith and

not by sight—were it possible for us to know, and knowing, properly appreciate the many privations they endured, the fatigue of body and anxiety of mind they experienced, we would gain insight into their characters that would surprise us. Not only have they performed some of the most daring deeds that have ever been recorded in history, but their constant unwavering devotion to the development of our country should excite in us feelings of gratitude and admiration. No class of women have a better right to be proud of their record. DeTocqueville never said of his own countrywomen what he said of ours. First, among the causes of their prosperity is the noble character of the American women, and I have faith to believe that as women, descended from such an origin, we will do something more than go out in a mere crush of fashionable luxury, folly and frivolous emptiness.

They may not stand out with as much individualism as did the women of the French Republic, but if they were excelled by them in dazzling and brilliant peculiarities, they have never darkened as they, the history of the past with deeds of blackness, and presented us with the appalling spectacle of a nation of virtueless women. Napoleon exclaimed what France most needs is mothers; we affirm what America *most* had *was mothers.* Let France then boast her females who excel in conversational talent and political intrigue, challenging the world to produce their superiors. Be this our boast that as true disinterested wives, loving, self-sacrificing mothers, and as women possessing the highest Christian attainments, the "Pioneer Women of the West" stand unrivaled. They were brave yet tender, encountering danger without compromising their gentleness. Forced in defense of themselves and little ones to wield at times weapons of death, they always preserved feelings keenly alive to distress and were swift to alleviate the disconsolate and oppressed.

We feel to-day we are treading holy ground. We come to chant a requiem over their tombs. To weave anew chaplets of fresh laurels for their graves. Their weary wayworn lives are ended—their toil-stained hands rest helplessly on pulseless bosoms—hands that were wont to press so tenderly the fevered brow. Their throbbing hearts are stilled forever—hearts whose loving sympathies made happy homes, the heavens on earth they were. God himself has wiped their tear stained eyes—eyes that grew dim with ceaseless vigils for their loves. Their tired feet are resting—feet that trod so faithfully life's thorny way, and yet the busy world moves on, while these, *our* dead, are almost forgotten, and we hear re-echoed this couplet, as though it might be their churchyard elegy,

"Full many a gem of purest ray serene,
The dark unfathomed caves of ocean bear,
Full many a flower is born to blush unseen,
And waste its sweetness on the desert air."

THE PIONEERS OF LICKING.

Read at the Pioneer Celebration at the Fair Grounds, Newark, Ohio, July 4th, 1872.

BY A. B. CLARK.

No wreath which we can weave to-day,
  Though Art and Science both combine;
No muse-inspired poet's lay,
  Though formed by all the heathen Nine:
No towering shaft—no marble urn,
  Inlaid with gold or filled with tears,
Are worthy incense now to burn,
  To Licking's honored Pioneers.

Love sets no lighter task for those,
  Who walk the paths their fathers trod;
Who worship where their songs uprose,
  From forest temples to their God,
Than this: to guard the well-earned fame,
  Of those who sowed mid toil and tears.
That we might harvest in the name,
  Of Licking's honored Pioneers.

Brave men were they, whose giant frames
  Were worthy types of Nature's skill;
Whose feats outranked Olympic games,
  Whose words were deeds—whose wish was will;
The forests fell beneath their blows,
  The flowers bloomed where'er they trod,
For them rich harvests waved—towns rose,
  And temples to the the living God.

Nor these alone the only lives,
　That well deserve our meed of praise;
Brave men require heroic wives,
　And such they had in those old days,
Who would have bared their arms beside,
　The proudest sculpture ever formed;
No man then sought a cotton bride,
　Nor one by Grecian bend deformed.

We may not call each honored name,
　Nor well recount each wondrous deed,
By which a wilderness was made,
　A blooming vale, a flowering mead;
With them no man was more than peer,
　But all were brothers heart and hand,
Strangers alike to awe or fear,
　Proud sovereigns of this western land.

No low born pride of caste or sect,
　Found lodgment in their fearless hearts;
No dualistic forms of faith,
　Could draw those noble men apart;
Each offered each an open palm,
　In joy or sorrow, toil or tears;
None failed to find a brother man,
　In Licking's noble Pioneers.

The wolves howled round their dwellings, and
　The wolf of want was sometimes there;
But in those humble cabin homes,
　Was Abrahamic faith and prayer;
Forests receded at their touch,
　Vines grew enriched by woman's tears;
We eat the fruit, and little think
　How much we owe those Pioneers.

Scorn not the hand made hard by toil,
　Ye dreamers in the lap of Ease;
Those iron-muscled iron men,
　Who felled your primal forest trees,

Were more than peers of Luxury's sons,
  Who revel in their wealth to-day,
And shun the hardy son of toil,
  Clad in his frock of hodden-gray.

Go ask the toilers of the field,
  The workers in your shops and mills,
The brawny arms that wield the axe,
  The horny hands that plough your hills;
Go ask of these what honored sons
  Of Licking we should most revere;
With one accord they make reply;
  "Remember Licking's Pioneer."

Ask who of all our race have shown,
  The largest heart the kindliest hand;
Ask who with lavish hands have strown,
  Rich blessings over all the land;
Ask who has sown that we might reap,
  The harvest rich with seventy years;
And every heart and every voice
  Makes answer: "Licking's Pioneers."

But now our hardy Pioneer
  Has laid his trusty rifle by;
For peace and plenty crowns the year,
  And age has dimmed the hunter's eye;
The music of the spinning wheel,
  Beside the hearth is heard no more,
For side by side the patriots kneel,
  To listen for the boatman's oar.

So go we back this Summer day,
  To memories of the olden time;
So seek to gild our simple lay,
  With words and deeds almost divine;
So pay our deference to gray hairs,
  The added wisdom born of years,
And hope on Heaven's altar stairs,
  To meet these same old Pioneers.